DEMONS

by
Donald R. Jacobs

An
Examination
of
Demons
at
Work
in the
World Today

HERALD PRESS, SCOTTDALE, PENNSYLVANIA

DEMONS: An Examination of Demons at Work in the World Today
Copyright © 1972 by Herald Press, Scottdale, Pa. 15683
International Standard Book Number: 0-8361-1666-6
Printed in the United States

Preface

I suppose a Preface written for a booklet such as this should be an attempt to prove the sanity of the author. In an age of nuclear physics, behavioral psychology, and interplanetary travel, it seems like a throwback to see a title like "Demons" and take it with a straight face.

Perhaps I shall be forgiven if I hasten to say that I have been a Christian missionary in Tanzania and Kenya since 1954. Missionaries are generally allowed to be slightly different because they are often influenced by the strange people they live among. So they are not treated quite like ordinary men. For instance, after I delivered a lecture on this subject to an American audience, one astute listener responded, "I actually think you may believe that demons are real." I nodded my head after which he produced a rather condoling smile. Christian brotherhood is very tolerant.

But if sanity is to be questioned, perhaps it should be directed to the John F. Funk Lectureship Committee who asked me to write this essay in the first place and, in fact, defined the subject for me. As far as I know, the committee members are all normal Christians.

Removing tongue from cheek, I must admit that my experience as a missionary and an anthropologist living among East African peoples has had a profound influence upon my thinking. In fact, I have come to appreciate deeply their view of life, especially as it regards the nature and activity of the spiritual forces in the universe. When I look at Jesus and the writings of the New Testament through their eyes, an entirely new light is thrown upon the message of the gospel. For this I shall be ever grateful. But I find that my experience is not unique. Many people in the West also find that without a profound understanding of the nature and activity of spirits, life remains an unsolvable riddle.

And I believe sincerely that the Funk Lectureship Committee could not have chosen a more pertinent topic for consideration because it is becoming an issue that is as contemporary as morning news, and for many is considered much more consequential.

This essay deals specifically with an analysis of demons as but one category of spirits. There are other categories, to be sure, but a study of demons is a helpful starter. This essay is only an introduction, and I sincerely hope that it will add to a proper understanding of the demonic powers and will stimulate others who are better equipped to "discern the spirits" than I to undertake serious study of the nature and activity of spiritual powers.

I want to thank the Funk Lectureship Committee for giving me the privilege of sharing my experience and views on this controversial and timely subject.

Donald R. Jacobs
September 30, 1971

DEMONS

This world is not easy to understand. The Apostle Paul talks about seeing through a darkened glass. There is movement, to be sure, as we squint our eyes to get a better look, but we find it very difficult to put it all together and make sense of it. Plato likened our experience to seeing distorted shadows cast by flames on the wall of a cave. We see a very small bit of reality and even that is confusing.

Thus the eternal question is still being asked in this enlightened age, Why do things happen the way they do? Science gives us some help in seeking simple causation; natural laws must be obeyed and all nature is subject to them. Science explains why objects fall down and why energy is another form of matter, but it really does not help much if we ask the questions: Why did the student want to drop the book? Why did the arsonist burn the barn?

Even though the answers to these "why" questions are difficult to obtain, we are not left bereft of wits on the earth. God gave us ears to hear, eyes to see, and the capacity to deduce and to assume that something is, even though we do not seem to know all the facts.

What a surprise we would have if we could see clearly all forces which are acting upon mankind at this very moment! Not every man necessarily has an angel on his one shoulder whispering good things into his ear and a devil on the other, but I do believe that we would be astounded if we could see only for a moment how men are being influenced by spiritual personalities in the world. The most urgent problem is not to seek causes within a closed mechanistic system but to look beyond nature to spiritual reality which must certainly be the ultimate cause. We must once again do research in the realm of the spirits. This is an ancient vocation, to be sure, but its antiquity need not deter us.

If there is more to life than meets the eye, then we should lose no time in searching for meaning and causative influences where we suspect they are. What makes things happen? The least scientific explanation is: "It is all chance, you know." Yet this is about all the thought we give to life. It is little wonder we are so ill-equipped to meet its demands.

This book attempts to examine one of the spiritual phenomena, demonology. Not only is demonology a recurring phenomenon in religious and cultural history, it is also a current reality for most of mankind today. In the following pages I want to examine the belief in demons in the biblical record and in our time with the hope that some of the confusion surrounding the existence of demons will be removed.

I write also as a Christian concerned that Christian men and women can confront demonic influences with some knowledge. Far too long Christians have been fighting the wrong battles. In Africa, where I live, we have made war against ignorance, disease, and poverty, all very good enemies for Christian men to fight, but we have not been very successful in confronting demonic powers. Jesus met them head on and dealt with them. Maybe, like Don Quixote, we are battling with windmills while the enemy goes about his plundering unchecked.

Furthermore, there are indications in the West that a religious era has already begun. The idea of demonic power as a causative influence is once again a live option in a culture which could not find its answers in materialistic scientism. Christians, of all people, should give careful attention to a study of the nature of demonic activity.

Demonology in the Bible

Biblical writers did not explain in too great detail what demons are and how they operate. However, biblical writers believed that demons existed. There is no doubt on this point. Furthermore, the belief in demons accompanies the belief in a personal, active devil.

The Old Testament does not record much about demonic activity. When it does so, it appears confusing at first glance. We usually think of demons as the devil's henchmen in the world and it comes as something of a shock to realize that in every instance where "evil spirit" is mentioned in the Old Testament, it is being "sent" by God and not Satan. In Judges 9 "God sent an evil spirit between Abimelech and the men of Shechem" to incite envy between them. They were allies in the murder of the seventy sons of Jerubbaal. Abimelech suffered very much due to this act of Providence and, in fact, perished in war which resulted from this evil spirit.

The other three instances have to do with Saul, the king. We read, "Now the Spirit of the Lord departed from Saul, and an evil spirit from the Lord tormented him."[1]

And further on we read, "An evil spirit from God rushed upon Saul, and he raved within his house."[2] And, "An evil spirit from the Lord came upon Saul, as he sat in his house with his spear in his hand."[3]

In these passages there is a consistency of method and purpose. God was displeased because of Abimelech's mass murder and Saul's arrogance and paranoidal fear of losing his throne. It is conceivable that God could have revealed His will in positive ways as He had often done, but in these instances He chose rather to permit evil to highlight a point He was trying to make with His people. (See Job 1:6-12.) The evil spirits, in these instances, produced ultimate good, even though their methods were quite evil.

That is about the extent of the recorded specific activity of evil spirits in the Old Testament, but there are many references to the evils of demon worship. While in Egypt, the Jews mixed with people who had demon cults. These cults were probably associated with the fertility cults in which images such as bulls and calves were prominent. After leaving Egypt, they came into contact with the many Semitic tribes in Arabia where they no doubt added to their already considerable knowledge of demons. Moses saw this as a very serious problem, so much so that he included it in his farewell song to his people. He hymned, "They sacrificed to demons which were no gods, to gods they had never known."[4]

Upon entering the promised land, they disobeyed God, mingled with the nations already there, and continued their cultic practices, no doubt enhanced by their increased traffic with the local people. David deplores this in Psalm 106. "They did not destroy the peoples, as the Lord commanded them, but they mingled with the nations and learned to do as they did. They served their idols, which became a snare to them. They sacrificed their sons and their daughters to the demons."[5]

The lack of frequent references to specific demonic activity in the Old Testament should not be taken to mean that little was known about it; on the contrary, it was widespread and needed no exposition. The Old Testament writers were, however, very unequivocal on one point: God-fearing men were not helpless before demonic onslaughts.

Before going on to examine the New Testament references, the question as to the possible origin of demons is in order. The Bible is not too explicit about the origin of demons. This fact has encouraged some men to speculate. One theory has it that in pre-Adamic times the earth was inhabited by men who rose up in rebellion against God and suffered as a consequence by having their material bodies removed, but their spirits remained. Now they exist as demons seeking hosts among the present race of men.[6] The glue which holds this theory together is not very strong.

Another explanation is that demons are the result of sexual intercourse between the angels and antediluvian women.[7] This theory is quite old, going back at least to the second century before Christ. The "Book of Enoch" is explicit about this.[8] The problem is, the "sons of God" may not be the same as the "angels of God," even though they are confused in the Septuagint. And who the "daughters of men" are is also not at all clear.

A correct theory of the origin of demons does not help much when it actually comes to dealing with demonic forces. Knowing where they came from neither adds nor subtracts from their evil deeds.

Unlike the Old Testament, demons often appear in the pages of the New Testament. They were well understood and highly feared at the time of Christ. Jesus had dialogue with them and the witnesses seemed to understand what was happening. Demon activity was common, just like it is in most of the world today. For this reason there was no need for a chapter on "demonology."

The Gospel writers record six specific exorcisms performed by Jesus. They are: The demoniac at Capernaum (early in Jesus' ministry), Luke 4; "Mary, called Magdalene, from whom seven demons had gone out," Luke 8; two Gadarenes in whom the "Legion" of the spirits dwelt, Luke 8; the blind and dumb demoniac, Matthew 12; the Canaanite woman's daughter, Matthew 15; a dumb demoniac, Matthew 9; and the lad whose possession took the form of epilepsy, Matthew 17. But there were also many others referred to *en masse*. "In that hour he cured many of diseases and plagues and evil spirits."[9] "They brought him . . . demoniacs."[10] "That evening they brought to him many who were possessed with demons; and he cast out the spirits with a word."[11]

In each case the demonic powers were making their hosts uncomfortable, in some cases producing most extraordinary behavior and in others just sickness. But the cause was recognized as

11

demonic activity. When Jesus confronted the demons, they immediately recognized Him and obeyed when commanded to leave the host. After the demons were exorcised, the hosts exhibited normal behavior. In no instance did Jesus pamper a demon. Mk 5 ?

Jesus touched on the nature and activity of demons Himself when He was speaking of the generation which was about to disown Him. He predicted for them a terrible judgment because they were about to reject Him, He who was greater than Jonah and Solomon. He could foresee for them a terrible end. It was in this context that He said: "When an unclean spirit comes out of a man it wanders over the deserts seeking a resting-place; and finds none. Then it says, 'I will go back to the home I left.' So it returns and finds the house unoccupied, swept clean, and tidy. Off it goes and collects seven other spirits more wicked than itself, and they all come in and settle down; and in the end the man's plight is worse than before. That is how it will be with this wicked generation."[12]

Jesus is warning them of something they had already experienced in part. Demons do exist. They take up residence in personalities which are properly prepared for them. By rejecting the Son of God the "wicked generation" unwittingly prepare themselves for an invasion of demonic influences.

Only a few days before His death, Jesus is even more vehement in His warnings: "O, Jerusalem, Jerusalem, thou that killest the prophets and stonest them which are sent unto thee, how often would I have gathered thy children together, even as a hen gathereth her chickens under her wings, and ye would not! Behold, your house is left unto you desolate."[13]

While this is not an exposition on the nature of demonic activity, Jesus is clarifying some very important things about demons. They are clearly associated with the anti-God forces in the world. They take up residence in places which are, in a sense, vacant, that is, in which there are no forces stronger than they are. They move in where there is pronounced weakness. The Revelator has caught this particular characteristic of demons when he describes the aftermath of the terrible and utter destruction of Babylon. He speaks in the Spirit, "Fallen, fallen is Babylon the great! It has become the dwelling place of demons, a haunt of every foul spirit."[14] Where dissipation has taken place, where the place has been swept clean but not filled with positive power — faith, hope, love, and the presence of Jesus — the demons reinhabit with delight.

The Apostle Paul encountered demonic powers in his ministry. He wrote to the Corinthian Church, "I imply that what pagans sacrifice they offer to demons and not to God.

I do not want you to be partners with demons. You cannot drink the cup of the Lord and the cup of demons. You cannot partake of the table of the Lord and the table of demons."[15] And James assured his readers that "even the demons believe — and shudder."[16]

It is abundantly clear that demons are included in the disobedient beings who are working against God and His purposes. They evidently assist any anti-Christly powers, even governments which oppress people and thwart justice. The Apostle John sees them actually promulgating the day of reckoning between the forces of the obedient and the disobedient. "I saw three unclean spirits come out of the mouth of the beast . . . the dragon . . . and the false prophet. . . . They are the spirits of demons doing signs who go abroad to the kings of the whole world, to assemble them for battle on the great day of God the Almighty. . . . And they assembled them at the place which is called in Hebrew Armageddon."[17] Demons are there to encourage evil rulers. There may be some sly humor in Jesus' response to the Pharisees' suggestion that He leave town before Herod gets hold of Him. He retorted, "Go and tell that fox, 'Behold, I cast out demons.'"[18]

It is not at all easy to construct a convincing demonology from these references from Scriptures. To make observations as we have been doing is rather simple. But to see how the concept of demons fits into a world view which is meaningful is not at all easy; however, this is what we shall attempt.

Christians are expected to make several assumptions. One is that God is, that we know most perfectly who He is through His Son Jesus of Nazareth, that Satan is the chief of the disobedient ones, and that he has considerable control over much that happens in the land of the living. The belief in beings, good and evil, follows from these few presuppositions. To believe in a personal presence of God among us, that is the Holy Spirit, should be no easier for us to believe than that there should be a personal devil who seeks to frustrate God's good designs for man. To assume a devil leads to the reasonable assumption that he has spirits or beings subject to him. These obedient and disobedient spirits clash on a cosmic scale and mankind is caught in the colossal struggle.

If these assumptions are correct, Satan has at his command powerful organizations to carry forward his evil plans. This is confirmed in the Scriptures where these systems or power structures are called principalities, powers, authorities, powers of the air, dominion of darkness. God, through Christ and the Spirit, has an organization of powers as well. We read of angels, of Michael the chief of the angels, and others. When Jesus rebuked Peter for cutting off the ear of one of the high priest's servants, He asserted that He could appeal to the Father and have more than twelve legions at His disposal.

To catch the full impact of the victory of Jesus Christ, life must be seen primarily in the context of cosmic tensions set up by the operation of these two opposing power organizations. This explains the absolute exhilaration which the disciples felt when they discovered that the demons were helpless before the "name" of Jesus. They had no doubt seen demons managed by the cultists, but in the name of Jesus demons actually fled. Something had happened in the power complexes in the realm of the spirits. Jesus was master of the demons! If the balance of power had swung to the side of Jesus and the obedient spirits, then all things were possible through His name. Prayer, seen in this light, became a blessed experience. And the power that this gave for evangelism and testimony was electrifying.

Jesus wanted His followers to have no doubt about the effect His life, death, and resurrection have on the balance of spiritual powers. When the disciples returned with joy announcing that the demons were subject to them in the name of Jesus, the Lord reported very matter-of-factly, "I saw Satan fall like lightning from heaven."[19]

This sounds very much like what John is

talking about in Revelation 12. He writes: "Now war arose in heaven, Michael and his angels fighting against the dragon; and the dragon and his angels fought, but they were defeated and there was no longer any place for them in heaven. And the great dragon was thrown down, that ancient Serpent, who is called the Devil and Satan, the deceiver of the whole world — he was thrown down to the earth and his angels were thrown down with him. And I heard a loud voice in heaven saying, 'Now the salvation and power and the kingdom of our God and the authority of his Christ have come, for the accuser of our brethren has been thrown down, who accuses them day and night before our God. And they have conquered him by the blood of the Lamb and by the word of their testimony, for they loved not their lives even unto death. Rejoice then, O heaven and you that dwell therein! But woe to you, O earth and sea, for the devil has come down to you in great wrath, because he knows his time is short.' "[20] Whether this is a prediction of some future event or whether it has already happened has caused considerable debate among Christian men of goodwill. But there is little debate on the central fact, that Jesus has in fact done something to upset the balance of power, a fact which marks the beginning of a new age.

This victory seems to have been paramount in Paul's thinking. "He disarmed the principalities and powers," he writes to the Colossians, "and made a public example of them, triumphing over them in him."[21] This is military language and speaks of the victory of one power over another. We can all but see Jesus proclaiming victory throughout the land. He has defeated the dragon Himself and inflicted him with a wound from which there is no recovery. The initiative is now His. He made "peace through the blood of his cross . . . whether they be things in earth, or things in heaven."[22] The good news is the simple fact that Jesus has overcome the one who had been holding captive the souls of men and now through His finished work, He can announce without equivocation, as He did in prophecy at the beginning of His ministry in Nazareth, "He has sent me to proclaim release to the captives . . . to set at liberty those who are oppressed."[23] On the very next Sabbath in a nearby town, Capernaum, He proved by action His word of prophecy. "In that synagogue there was a man who had the spirit of an unclean demon; and he cried out with a loud voice, 'Ah! What have you to do with us, Jesus of Nazareth? Have you come to destroy us? I know who you are, the Holy One of God.' " Jesus ordered the demon out and the worshipers were "amazed and said to one another, 'What is this Word? For with authority and power he commands the unclean spirits, and they come out.' "[24] The casting out of demons was an act which had crucial importance to the witness of Jesus Christ, for it proved without doubt that His power exceeded the power of the enemy. And, after all, is that not the significance of Christ's total work? Is this not the reason He is able to forgive sin, to change men, and draw the disobedient to Himself?

The Pharisees had trouble understanding Jesus. They assumed that when the Messiah would come, He would elevate the law and for all intents and purposes look and act like a Pharisee. They managed to argue their way through His theology, but they could not deny that He displayed extraordinary power by casting out demons. They finally solved the riddle and it was so simple. Jesus, they said, could undoubtedly cast out demons. This fact was demonstrated time and time again. But He was able to do this, they said, because He was given power by the prince of the demons, Beelzebub. But Jesus asked them a very disturbing question, "If I cast out demons by Beelzebub, by whom do your sons cast them out? Therefore they shall be your judges. But if it is by the finger of God that I cast out demons, then the kingdom of God has come upon you."[25] Here Jesus again puts the coming of the kingdom of God into the context of a victory. The kingdom is because Jesus has in fact become King. And the fact that He is

King is demonstrated in His ability to **cast out** demons and to forgive sin. Jesus goes on to explain what is happening using another, slightly different figure. "No one can enter a strong man's house and plunder his goods, unless he first binds the strong man; then indeed he may plunder his house."[26] Jesus was certainly plundering the house of the enemy! He was setting His prisoners free and proclaiming liberty to the captives. Previous to this Satan had possessed his goods in peace, being the strongest on earth.

It is in this context of asserting His newly won victory that Jesus cast out demons, healed the sick, and forgave sin. Leinstad believes that Jesus viewed His activity as exorcist and healer in a messianic, eschatological perspective. A careful reading of the text confirms this observation.

We can draw conclusions from the foregoing. Jesus cast out demons, healed the sick, and forgave sin, all indicating that He worked the works of His Father. As far as demons are concerned, and that is the focus of this study, their mention in the pages of the New Testament is not incidental. It is not as though Jesus ran across the phenomenon here and there and finally decided He had to do something about it. On the contrary, casting out demons was a crucial, if not an indispensable, part of His ministry. His dialogue with the demons and His power over them laid bare the central facts of His incarnational victory over the enemy of men's souls. He could spoil the enemies' goods and He did.

Demon Activity Today

In most of the world, the phenomenon of demon-possession resembles that of the New Testament. Here is an account written in 1970 by a Kenyan female schoolteacher:

> There was a woman who was possessed and she was at the point of running mad. Her husband, Mr. Mwasi, spent almost all he had with the *waganga* [local practitioners], but the woman could not get healed. Instead she became worse. Finally, the husband despaired and decided to call some of the people whom he heard claim they could lay hands on the sick and the sick would recover. So we went and it was night. In the house we sang to God and then the moment of prayer came. Somehow the demons in her were troubled and she started jumping up and down and shouting very loudly, she then fell down and fainted. Then the Spirit of God talked through me saying, "Keep quiet all of you and let each pray silently." We obeyed the Spirit and after a moment of silence for about five minutes, the woman suddenly shut up and said she had some things she kept for the demons. So she climbed up to the *kai* [this is a big shelf above the fireplace in a round house where we store maize and other things] and brought down a lot of medicines from the *waganga* and some small things. She also untied from her waist a piece of cloth she had bought especially for these

demons. After that, we cast out the demons in the name of Jesus and she became well from that time to this day. The next day we burnt all the things which she had brought out.

The incidence of demon-possession is certainly not diminishing in Africa. Rev. L. Swantz, a missionary living in Dar es Salaam, Tanzania, writes,

> On the Tanzania coast where I live, hardly a night goes by without the sound of the madogoli drums which is a sign that medicine men, drummers, and the village and lineage members are expelling a spirit and trying to find out what it desires. These are not isolated events, but indications that animism, with its spirit-possession cults, plays a very large role in the life of the people. It is not dying out, except in the urban areas, but even there the urban dwellers return to the country for the spirit rites.[27]

As far as I know, no one has tried to find out the extent of demon-possession in any ethnic group in Africa, but the general impression one gets through reading and experience indicates that it shows no signs of decline. In the tribes with which I am acquainted, the frequency of possession is not constant but varies. At times it sweeps an entire community and then subsides. There is certainly an element of suggestibility in possession which makes it "catching." On the other hand, demon activity may be greater at one time than at another for the simple reason that demons are more active at some times than at others in a particular locality.

Some people believe that demonic activity was peculiar to the time when Jesus walked the earth. That may have been a period of intense activity but the identical phenomenon is recognizable now in practically every culture. Demons have been in existence for a long time.

There has been so much confusion on the entire concept of demons in modern times that it is quite impossible to carry on an intelligent conversation unless some definitions are given. We, therefore, turn to the phenomenon as it now is to determine the nature and work of demons.

We find anthropological literature especially helpful. As a resident of Kenya, my firsthand knowledge comes, of course, from the African world but fairly wide reading has convinced me that there are some common features the world over.

There are some negative generalizations to begin with — what demons are not. They are not the spirits of the ancestral dead. Many of the world's folk religions hold to the following beliefs. The departed dead continue to communicate with the living for a generation or more and reveal themselves through mediums, through extraordinary acts such as sickness and sterility, or through straightforward appearances such as in dreams or even on the path. These disincarnate ancestors seldom reside in the living, unless, of course, there is a reincarnation in which case the spirit of the ancestor is in fact the spirit of the person. But these spirits can reside for periods of time in natural objects or animals. Their primary duty is to perpetuate the group and bring blessing and judgment as they are able.

Many societies believe that the ancestral spirits are the great invisible police force and omnipresent judges who keep the living walking the straight and narrow way of the tribe. The demons have no such functions. The "ghost" phenomenon is usually associated with the spirits of the dead and not with demons. However, there are references to people "hearing" demons crying and shouting in desolate places, but they are rarely seen.

Furthermore, it is believed that demons do not usually share the value system of the group. They are considered foreign spirits. That is one reason they are so hard to understand or control. Ancestral spirits appear to respond to sacrifices, offerings, and moral reformation on the part of the living.

Demons do not seem to work toward disrupting the fabric of society as do the evil ancestral spirits. Yet demons are usually thought of as evil because they will harm the people they inhabit unless their demands are met. Let the young lady who was quoted earlier describe the activity of these demons in her tribe:

Traditionally the Wataita [my tribe] believed in spirits which had power to inhabit individuals and places like houses and forests. It was very strongly believed that individuals got possessed by these spirits unwillingly. The spirits demanded certain things from the victim. If she failed to fulfill the wish of the spirit, she or he became very ill until she acted accordingly. All spirits demanded that the victim go to *Ngomenyi*, that is a dance where only drums are used occasionally.

Other things the spirits demanded varied depending on the individual spirit for they had various names like Mzuka, Dungumale, Jini, and Mwasindika. Some of the things demanded are: red clothes, black clothes, white clothes, mouth organs, hats, some gods, the victim to eat the flesh of a dog, snails, soil, and many other nasty things.

These spirits manifested themselves in sickness, madness, the victim acting in a very funny way, dancing vigorously, jumping, shouting, and speaking in an ecstatic way and the person shakes very vigorously. Sometimes the person faints, especially when she goes to *Ngomenyi*.

One of these spirits [more than one can inhabit an individual] shouts very loudly anywhere, even in the middle of a conversation or a meal!! Well, nervous people have to be careful lest they get shocked. Such was and still is the traditional belief in spirits. The only cure is to give them what they demand.

Demons are restless, homeless spirits who must inhabit people in order to get what they want. And if they do not get what they are after, they can torment the poor subject mercilessly, causing sickness, temporary insanity, or just plain nastiness. A husband or wife who is being pestered by a demon is almost impossible.

There are three major types of demon-possessions which might be called demon-taming, demon-dominance, and soul-stealing. In the first instance, a demon may in fact be secretly welcomed by a prospective host for some selfish reason and, therefore, move in, or it may move into a host as an unwelcome intruder. The host, in either case, must deal with the demon's presence. Usually the local demon cults become aware of the situation and their services are made available, for a fee. They will assist the host to understand what the demon demands and how to satisfy it. If the demon is not overly demanding and if the host can continue to meet the demands of the demon, a kind *modus vivendi* is established wherein both host and demon live in a symbiotic relationship. An arrangement such as this can go on for years.

However, demons are demons after all and once they have a position in a host, they may invite fellow demons in or may become overly demanding and cause great trouble. This situation can lead to another type of possession in which case the demons dominate the host's personality either all or part of the time. If this occurs, the cults will probably try to exorcise the demon or demons lest the host be killed. The power to exorcise does not reside in the human will alone; therefore, forces stronger than that of the demon must be sought. Handling powers of this kind is a very dangerous business and only a few brave souls dare get involved as the risks are very high. In many societies, exorcisms of this type are not even attempted because the power which is necessary to exorcise could well dominate the exorcists. The hosts are simply excluded from communal life and avoided by all sensible men.

The third type of possession occurs when the demons make off with a man's soul and if the cultists cannot get it back within a reasonable length of time, usually within twenty-four hours, the host's body will die of entropy. This is especially typical of demonic activity in Latin America where the "souless state" is called *susto*.

In all cases of possession, the will of the host experiences the presence of a counter will which often acts in a way which is contrary to the host's welfare.

There are many sociological and psychological factors in demonic activity. We shall touch on only a few of them.

A very knowledgeable anthropologist working on the East African coast, Dr. M. Swantz, is finding that demonism seems to grow as a group's fears grow. When a group is under pressure from a variety of sources, the demons are overly active. The demons are usually identified with the disruptive forces! At the present time, the demons often ask for European things and might, therefore, be associated with European spirits. Europeans are, of course, the great disruptors in East Africa.

In passing, it may be interesting to note that it is conceivable that a woman, for instance, who is having difficulty getting something she needs out of a stingy husband might seek, or at least welcome, possession and claim that her demon demands a nice piece of cloth which she, incidentally, needs for a new dress. Owing to husband's perennial suspicion, however, if this is a trick, it cannot be played too often.

To possess a demon, or rather to be possessed by one, is not always a socially unacceptable state. In societies in which the possession of extraordinary psychic power is desirable, the added power resulting from the possession is desirable, if the demon can be satisfied. But the demon's demands can be very high. However, it enhances a person's status so much that he pays willingly. When a demon's demands cannot be met, however, then the situation deteriorates and the angry demon expresses dissatisfaction by bringing about every kind of misfortune.

However, under normal conditions, many societies can tolerate a high incidence of demon-possession, especially if demon cults are in operation. This requires some explanation as demon cults are very important for the smooth operation of society. In many East African tribes, if a person has an overly demanding demon whose desires cannot be met or if the community discovers that the person has a demon, then attempts must be made to come to terms with the demon or the demons are actually exorcised. The exorcists are generally not the traditional doctors but are those who have themselves been possessed and have experienced demonic possession. These people form clubs. Their deeds are dark and mysterious. This is because they must, of course, have power to communicate with demons and they realize that this power must come from without themselves. They, therefore, must have secret alliances with other powers which they can call upon to accomplish their ends. These demon cults study demon phenomena and manipulate powers in order to either satisfy, domesticate, or exorcise the demons. It can readily be seen that the members of these cults live very dangerously because in order to obtain the power to confront demons in a meaningful way, they must strike bargains with these awesome powers. Those who deal with demons are, therefore, in turn highly feared and also highly honored.

Some cults revere a few very powerful demons who can drive out others, something like the Pharisees' reference to casting out demons by the power of the great demon, Beelzebub. Often there is one great male and a great female demon to which the cult owes allegiance and which they in fact exalt. This produces a situation which could actually be called "demon worship," in which case offerings and sacrifices are made to these great spirits and the cultists stand in great awe of their power. When the Apostle Paul warns against worshiping demons and "elemental spirits," he is probably referring to this kind of worship.

But why should one person be possessed and another not? Does possession have any rhyme or reason? In his research in Hong Kong, P. M. Yap found that for possession to occur, the subject must be dependent and conforming in character. He will probably occupy a position in society that does not allow the person reasonable opportunity for self-assertion and the person must be confronted with a problem which he sees no hope of solving.[28]

This theory is supported by evidence from Africa. For instance, if a junior wife is overshadowed by senior wives or other strong persons, she may be especially open to the possibility of enhancing her status by flirting with a demon. It may be her only recourse to a source of power. Or a person in the community who feels himself ignored or neglected can gain recognition very quickly by hosting a demon.

A normal individual who is coping well with his environment and relationships in socially acceptable patterns or a person who is getting the power he needs to defend himself against his adversaries in some way or another is not the kind of person a demon would expect to inhabit. Demons need more hospitable conditions than that. They move in when and where conditions are suitable. They respond to invitations which arise from desperation or move in entirely on their own. For this reason, demon-possession has often been associated with mental disorders. For a time, some powerless people do find a certain identity through "pampering" a demon but the end is often worse than the beginning.

In societies where the place and power of women is minimal, it is to be expected that female demon-possession should be more frequent than male possession. This seems to hold true in East Africa, where possession is strongest in Islamized societies, where women have traditionally been almost second-class citizens. In traditional Bantu society, women had much more power than under Muslim law and, therefore, had less need to hanker after demonic power.[29]

This, then, is a summary of some of the major features of the demon phenomenon as found in today's world. Should this be of any concern to Christians? Is this an area of life which godly men should avoid? Does it have any bearing at all upon evangelism in our time?

Demons and Evangelism

As far as I know, there are no mission churches in Africa which practice exorcisms. Why this should be is very difficult to discover. But I imagine the most immediate reason is that by actually practicing exorcism, a certain credence is given to the whole idea of spirit-possession. The nonofficial missionary stance would be like Evans-Pritchard's attitude to witchcraft. The famous anthropologist wrote, "Witchcraft is an imaginary offence because it is impossible."[30] Most missionaries would say that demon-possession is simply superstition. In my own experience, the general feeling among missionaries is that even if there should be an exorcism ritual, it would simply be a farce because that which it seeks to exorcise does not exist. This would make a mockery of Christian ritualistic practices. How can you cast out a demon if you do not believe it exists?

Almost all Western missionaries are influenced by the thinking reflected in this statement found in the *International Standard Bible Encyclopedia:* "The term 'communion with demons' does not imply any power on the part of men to enter into voluntary relationship with beings of another world, but that, by sinful compliance in wrongdoing, such as idol worship and magical rites, men may enter into a moral identification with evil powers against which it is their duty to fight."[31] The meaning of this is not very clear, but it at least casts some doubt upon the reality of demons per se.

There was a benign assumption in the early days of missions in non-Western cultures that if no attention at all is given to a traditional phenomenon by the church, it will simply wither on the vine and die. In other words, forget about demons and they are not. The moment you cast one out, you are in effect announcing the authenticity of demons and when this happens, there is no telling what might come out of Pandora's box of surprises. It is best simply to turn a blind eye to this phenomenon and hope that it will soon go away like a bad dream in the morning.

The fault in this assumption lies in the simple fact that the phenomenon is not about to vanish. In fact, it has persisted with growing frequency. Parrinder notes with reference to witchcraft, "There is little sign of a decrease in witchcraft belief with increasing education."[32] The same could be said of the belief in demons.[33]

At this point, it may be helpful to make a definitive distinction between witchcraft and demon activity. Witchcraft has a relational base. It is the process of one rational being

33

willing evil against another. Witchcraft takes many forms, but in every case it is anti-social. When witchcraft activity is intense, the entire social fabric is in danger of disintegrating. Demons might be socially disruptive, but this is not their intention. A society which believes in witchcraft finds it easy to believe in demons, and vice versa, but the two are separate and distinct in practice. Witches are not simply people who have demonic power at their disposal.

The New Testament is almost entirely silent about witches. Parrinder makes the observation, "In the New Testament there is not a trace of belief in witches, unless they are to be vaguely included under the general catalogue of the works of the flesh, idolatry, sorcery, enmities."[34] Demon activity, however, is prominent in the New Testament.

Is it possible that great harm has been done to the cause of Christ because demonology was not considered respectable during the modern mission era? The answer to this question is probably "yes," because generally speaking people convert to another faith because they are seeking more power. What power did the people in the non-Western world see and desire in the missionary? More than likely it had to do with the fact that he represented a very powerful culture with advanced technology, education, and weaponry and not because of the power of Christ which defeated the demonic forces.

Is this not a tragic misrepresentation of the essence of the Christian faith? It would not have been so bad if the recipients of the gospel had had no concept of spirits and demons. But in Africa, Latin America, and Polynesia, the world view of the people resembles that of the New Testament world, a world populated with spirits. Jesus proved His lordship by becoming Lord of the spirits, exorcising demons, healing the sick, and forgiving sins. Modern missions dealt almost exclusively with the last, the "sin-forgiving" aspect of the faith. But the demons remained and they were exorcised, as they had been for centuries past, by traditional practices. Christian faith, therefore, had its limits. What Christ was not expected to do, the local practitioners could! Not only did this produce a truncated faith in many instances, but it was an appeal to faith on the wrong premise — the power of Western culture rather than the power of Jesus Christ in the realm of the spirits.

By not introducing Jesus to all levels of spiritual beliefs in a culture, rationale is given to a sort of spiritual dualism in which Jesus answers some questions and other spiritual powers, others. The Christian faith cannot endure this state of affairs. There are some indications that this search for wholeness, to get all under the lordship of Christ, is at the root of the massive indigenization movement in Africa. If there is a common thread running through most of the indigenous African churches, it is this. And the Pentecostal movements in Latin America and the Far East may be the result of the same need. These new movements announce clearly that Jesus Christ is Lord of all, even the powers of evil spirits.

Demons and Western Culture

Granted, some would say, demons do function in the "less enlightened" areas of the world, the possibility of detecting demonic activity in the West is so remote that we should not waste precious time trying. This may or may not be true. Within the past decade or two, occultism has become a rather respectable preoccupation for certain kinds of people in Western societies. These groups are studying extraordinary phenomena and some are experimenting with the world of the spirits. This follows an era when it was assumed that when all of the secrets of the universe are told, we should not be surprised to find that only material forces have been at work after all. As someone prophesied, "There is less here than meets the eye."

Since World War II, however, some thoughtful men are beginning to doubt that basic assumption. Some psychologists, notably Jourard, rightfully question the assumption that all emotional malady is to be interpreted mechanistically. Some physical scientists are beginning to realize that when they deal with physical phenomena, they are touching but a small portion of reality. Some historians, especially those who are archaeologically oriented, detect movement, pattern, and function in the kaleidoscope of history which may be more than the simple imposition of the human mind ever seeking to find purpose. Materialistic assumptions are increasingly suspect.

This does not necessarily mean that Western man is once again ready to accept a god who is "way out there," in the Greek sense of the word, a god who inhabits the lofty heights of Mount Olympus. He seeks for God, not in the "other" world, but within what he already knows and experiences. Was it not an early missionary who said, "God is within you"?

While it is very dangerous to try to guess what is happening, is there not a certain mood of disenchantment about scientism in the Western world? Is it saying too much to assert that there is a movement out of the era of rationalism into something which may be called relationalism? Is this not what the prophets such as Bonhoeffer and other relational theologians began to see?

If there is indeed movement toward an age which will be known for its spiritual awakening, we can expect that many strange things will take place. When people who are theologically illiterate begin to dabble in matters of the spirit, anything can happen. When starved men finally eat, they may not be able to go about it with cool heads or ready stomachs.

If this is true, then Western culture is probably going to be increasingly interested in spiritual phenomena and there will certainly be renewed interest in the phenomenon of demons. For this reason, it may be helpful to assume for a moment that demons are in fact active, even now, in the Western world. After all, this should not be an impossible thought for Christians who profess to believe in spirits. Assuming demons are, we should know about their activity in Western cultures.

There once lived a skeptical fisherman who heard unbelievable stories about people catching fish two feet long; he had never got one over twelve inches. One day he caught one three feet long, held it by the tail, shook his head, threw it back into the water and said, "Just another lie." Likewise, faced with the evidence of a "real live demon" a Western man would probably react just about this way. "There just are no such things," he would say.

If we assume demons do exist and that they have some intelligence, they would be absolutely foolish to present themselves as demons to people who reject the whole idea. Intelligent demons would go about their business with others labels, other names. After all, who would be able to detect them (and exorcise them) if they simply encourage "compulsive status seeking," or chauvinistic patriotism, or nonpersonal scientism and materialism? They could get away with murder just because people do not detect what is happening.

Within the past century, psychiatrists have identified a veritable encyclopedia of psychopathological syndromes and the work is far from finished. We know more about what can go wrong mentally than any generation that ever lived. But is it not possible that this has been little more than an exercise of description? For ultimately the question remains, why do people have a tendency to pathological disintegration? And why does not everyone desire wholeness so fervently that disintegrating or eroding forces are given little chance? The answer to this question is to be found in the area of the will, where a person makes either positive or negative decisions about the business of living. If a person wholeheartedly wants to cope positively with life, then he will find ways and means of doing so. If, however, he finds it impossible to come to terms with reality in a positive way, he is opening himself to possible demonic activity after which he will find it very, very difficult to respond positively.

It is not a problem of how, in other words,

but of why. "Why should I affirm life? Why should I even want to have lasting relationships? Why should I love? Why doesn't society leave me alone? Why do I hate myself?" If these why-type questions are not answered, then the demons can move in and produce a variety of symptoms from schizophrenia to suicidal compulsion. The ultimate "why" question is, "Why ask why?" When this low ebb is reached, psychological and physical disintegration is at the door. Perhaps it is only at this point that we dare, even in the West, use the adjective "demented."

There comes a point at which a society can no longer tolerate someone with deviant behavior. When this point is reached, community forces are supposed to respond and press for some sort of reintegration. More traditional cultures have ways and means understood by all to bring this about, whether by exorcisms, putting the demented in touch with ancestral reality, or similar methods. In Western pluralistic cultures, "tribes" which can do this effectively seldom exist and one can stand lonely in a crowd. No one cares — until his deviant behavior causes others some hardship. Then society asserts itself and places him in the hands of the modern shaman, the psychiatrist. He is supposed to be convinced that there is some purpose in life, like personal fulfillment. This is not clear, so shock therapy may follow. Or failing all else, mechanistic behavior patterns are established like conditioning a person by an undesirable stimulus not to walk about naked. Some modicum of culturally acceptable behavior will probably follow, but if disintegration or entropy has reached this point, there is little hope that any spirit can again be breathed into the person.

It seems as though Western culture, with its ambivalence about matters of the spirit, is blind to the devastating effect of the demonic forces in the area of personality disintegration.

Sidney Jourard, a practicing psychiatrist, feels confident that something goes on at the center of the will which he calls inspiration, or spirit mobilization.[35] Jourard has the courage to assume that man has a spirit and that it can be influenced positively or negatively. Threatened by an invasion of germs, for instance, the spirit can say either, "Why struggle?" or "Sure, I can beat them off." And it is an observed fact that the people who have the will to fight an invading force have a better chance to survive than those who do not. The question is not whether the "hope syndrome" has determinative value; this is clear; but how can the "hope syndrome" be positively influenced?

According to Jourard, anything which can encourage hope has some positive effect. The highly educated doctor, for example, who, surrounded by learned books, dispenses his expensive medicines, has a great effect on patients. This is what is called the "placebo effect," which means that just experiencing meaningful symbols produces a positive effect in the spirit. Love can do this, as well as prayer. All of these things encourage the person's spirit to respond positively. It is this process of strengthening spirit that Jourard calls inspiritation.

Jourard has come to his conclusions by examining the relationship between a person's attitude about life and his power to recuperate. This is perhaps the most easily handled research situation. But if it is true that an American man has a spirit and that this spirit can be influenced both positively and negatively, either inspirited or despirited, there is very little difference between a Kenyan, we might say, and an American. The Kenyans' philosophical system is based upon this assumption. They, therefore, research the factors which inspirit and those which despirit. It is in this context that demons, witches, ancestral spirits, God, and the divinities are examined. Perhaps the greatest difference between African and Western approaches at this point is that Africans try to control the external forces causing either inspiriting or despiriting, while Western man looks at the system which is being affected and seeks to reorganize it from within. The result is that the African confronts demonic forces; Western man, not recognizing who they are, tries to accommodate them.

This is not to suggest that all mental demoralization is demonogenic, but if demons act consistently, it is precisely in the process of despiriting that their activity would be anticipated.

As in other cultures, in the West there may well be demon activity at a low-volume level in many cases which are experiencing demoralization or despiriting. As the situation deteriorates and the spirit is greatly weakened, the activity of the despiriting influences become even clearer. Therapy requires an equal inspiriting process to produce life-affirming forces. Said in theological terms, the demon presence must be exorcised and the person infilled with the Spirit of God who consistently affirms life. The Spirit of God has no suicidal tendencies.

If all of this is true, then some therapy is possible by simple placebo manipulation — that is, when someone is despirited for some reason or another, say because of an impossible boss or a nagging wife, he can be helped to regain his spirit by lying on the couch of a learned psychoanalyst or hearing some soothing words by a spiritual counselor in whom he has great confidence. Perhaps he can be made to see that the overdemanding boss or the sharp-tongued wife only appear to be so because there is something in himself which is threatened.

Therapy, therefore, requires an internal reorganization so that he is no longer threatened. This is how we inspirit one another all of the time. We are constantly trying to help one another to take a positive grip on life. Heaven knows there is enough going on around us to convince us that the only sensible approach is the opposite one, to say it is all absurd and give up; but something tells us that a negative view to life weakens our powers to live, and survive we must. There is no alternative, then, other than to affirm life and thus strengthen the will to be, the will to live. Jesus made it very clear that this is the correct stance, to affirm life every day. Therefore, we are all undergoing therapy all of the time.

The gnawing doubts about the worthwhileness of life are not godly thoughts. Whether they can be called demonic or not is not clear. But what does seem clear from a careful reading of the New Testament and anthropological literature is that when a person persists in life-denying thinking, he opens himself to the possibility of hosting a demon.

If this is true and if this point is reached, then ordinary therapy is not able to produce positive results. The demonic influence must be dealt with. And in dealing with demons a question of exorcism is faced, not simply one of inspiriting.

This now brings us full cycle. If demons

"are" and if they act in Western culture like they do in other cultures and if Western man is coming to realize the spiritual nature of the universe, then once again it may be that the most convincing immediate sign of Jesus Christ's lordship is His power to cast out the demons which are reinforcing life-denying attitudes in the West. Once again evangelism is back where it all started, where Jesus Himself confronts recognized demonic forces. Is it not possible to imagine that we are entering upon an era when there will be a major confrontation between Jesus Christ and the demonic forces in Western culture? There are signs which presage this.

Not only are demonic forces operating on a personal psychological level, they are also involved with influencing persons involved in power structures and institutions. Any institution where individuals persist in life-denying activities is wide open for demonic empowering, from the little exploiting business to vast institutions who do but lip service to justice and humanity. Any activity which dehumanizes people, even to the point of killing them, or which exploits resources and pollutes the environment without a thought given to the unborn potential sufferers is certainly anti-godly. Demons find such company hospitable.

We know much less about the activity of demonic forces at this level than at the individual level and, therefore, are less equipped to deal with them. But the same situation prevails — Jesus Christ has power and authority over demons because "he disarmed the principalities and powers."[36] And it is still true that "with authority and power he commands the unclean spirits, and they come out."[37]

Conclusion

A friend of mine who lives in a middle-class area of New Jersey reported that 30 percent of the space at the local magazine stand is given to periodicals on astrology, spiritism, the occult, and such like. This interest in seeking points of reference outside man is symptomatic of a lostness, a purposelessness. Jourard thinks, "By the time most of us reach adulthood, we have lost intimate contact with our actual selves."[38] When man is lost like this, he looks to the stars to find an answer to his dilemma, or he turns to drugs in order to refind reality, or to the occult to sink roots into a world of mystery. This restlessness of the spirit in the West is taking man on a new search for the meaning of life, a review of what the spiritual forces really are which pull and tug at the life of man. Western man feels caught in a life-denying culture which seems bent on self-destruction. Our greatest achievement, the bomb, is simply the most effective noose ever contrived by man. Who would have thought that the age of scientism would blossom in the production of a bigger and better gibbet?

Something has gone desperately wrong. We feel deeply that we must once again make peace with nature, peace with one another, with ourselves, and with God. We have lost faith in mechanistic methodology. We are beginning to feel as man has now and again felt ever since he was man, that ultimate reality must lie in the realm of the spirit. So a new research begins, into the world of the spirit. How ill-equipped we are for this new adventure! We had almost forgotten that the world of the spirit existed at all. It is like reentering a place we had been but the sights are strange and we have no map.

But it is an authentic search. And no one can go far before he encounters Jesus. Who is this Man? Is He wrong or is He really the King of kings and Lord of lords, the One who, through suffering and death, bore the sins of the penitent, broke the power of sin and hell and now sets men free to say "yes" to God and "yes" to life? Is He still the One who can, with authority and power, confront the demonic forces and command "Come out" and they come out? I believe He is.

Exorcism in Christ's Name

How should demons be identified and exorcised by the Christian community? While each instance of demon-possession and exorcism must be treated individually, there are some general guidelines which should be noted.

Do not be hasty in coming to the conclusion that the person is in fact hosting a demon. Study the Scriptures carefully to acquaint yourself with the signs of demon activity. And there is a further caution: do not confront demons alone. Always be in the company of other believers so that prayers and concerns can be shared. In each Christian fellowship, there should be one or more persons who have a special gift of discernment. This gift may not be obvious until circumstances arise which call for its exercise. It is good to allow those who have this gift to assist in determining whether or not a demon is involved.

Remember that demon-possession is quite rare. Do not think that simply because a certain temptation recurs a demon is involved. Demon-possession, as we have seen, is most likely after considerable moral decay has taken place. Recurrent temptation is common to all Christians and these are dealt with through repentance and cleansing by the poured-out lifeblood of Jesus. When there is compulsive and sustained desire to sin and an accompanying sense of defeat and failure which torments the hosts, perhaps the cause is demonic.

Insanity is in no way synonymous with demon-possession. Insanity can be organic in origin or can result from personality disintegration which is brought about by certain psychic disturbances. Demons find weakened personalities likely hosts, but that does not mean that all personalities so weakened are demon-possessed. Try to make sure through communal prayer and discussion that demon activity is in fact present.

In a fellowship of prayer, speak to the host and encourage him to confess his known sin, especially in the area where the moral weakening has taken place. The members of the fellowship must bind themselves to keep what is said in strict confidence. The fellowship should then identify the demon and with the laying on of hands command the demon in the name and power of Jesus Christ to come out. If the name of the demon is compulsive sexual lust, call him that. If it is a demon of kleptomania, call him that. Identify the demon. This is of primary importance.

If the host cannot respond, then speak directly to the demon. Ask who he is, how many there are, what they want, and then in the name of Christ cast them out. When the demon leaves, it is often the opportunity for the Holy Spirit to enter with great power. Pray for this believing that it is God's will that it be so.

The fellowship of prayer is no less meaningful after the demon has been cast out than before. Continue in fellowship with the former host. He can be a great witness to the grace of God in Christ. Furthermore, someone who has already hosted a demon is often the one who can, above all others, identify demonic activity in others. In the name of Jesus and within the context of the believing community his gifts can be put to use.

In the Christian walk provision is made for everything. A Christian need not fear that he will become demented as long as he has his heart open to Jesus Christ and the church. If he keeps alive the spirit of repentance and regularly reaffirms the lordship of Christ, he allows no door through which demons must enter.

Study and Discussion Questions

Jesus spoke often about love and the importance of love in Christian living. How can love assist the lover and the loved to cope with life? How can caring love become the normal Christian response to life's demands? Love is most effective in community. How can Christians rediscover caring, loving fellowship? Does congregational life encourage loving communion among the members?

Should there be an accepted exorcism ritual in the church? Should exorcism be considered a charismatic gift or should it be ritualized, like the wedding ceremony?

Much has been said about divine healing in the past few years. Are there various ways for Christian people to encourage positive health? Does being a committed Christian contribute to mental and physical health? Should the church take seriously her healing function? How can a Christian minister contribute to the good health of his congregation, or the Sunday school teacher to her class?

Are demons real or simply another way that people have discovered to transfer guilt to another being so that they do not need to carry it themselves? Does this fully explain the demon phenomenon?

Paul notes that "discerning the spirits" is a gift of the Spirit to the church. How does this gift express itself in a Western church? Is there need for this gift now?

Footnotes

1. 1 Samuel 16:14. Except as otherwise indicated, the references below are from the *Revised Standard Version of the Bible*, copyrighted 1946 and 1952 by the National Council of Churches and used by permission.
2. 1 Samuel 18:10.
3. 1 Samuel 19:9.
4. Deuteronomy 32:17.
5. Psalm 106:34-37.
6. This theory is explained in G. H. Pember's *Earth's Earliest Ages*, 1900.
7. Genesis 6:2, paraphrased.
8. "Book of Enoch," Ch. XV.
9. Luke 7:21.
10. Matthew 4:24.
11. Matthew 8:16.
12. Matthew 12:43-45. From *The New English Bible*. © The Delegates of the Oxford University Press and the Syndics of the Cambridge University Press, 1961, 1970.
13. Matthew 23:37, 38, KJV.
14. Revelation 18:2.
15. 1 Corinthians 10:20, 21.
16. James 2:19.
17. Revelation 16:13, 14, 16.
18. Luke 13:32.
19. Luke 10:18.
20. Revelation 12:7-12.
21. Colossians 2:15.
22. Colossians 1:20, KJV.
23. Luke 4:18 and Isaiah 61:1.
24. Luke 4:33-36.
25. Luke 11:19, 20.
26. Mark 3:27.
27. Rev. L., Swantz, *African Beliefs in Transition* (mimeo), p. 6.
28. P. M. Yap, "The Possession Syndrome," *Journal of Mental Science*, 106:114, 1960.
29. There is some intelligent speculation that demonism was not a highly developed cult in many parts of Africa until the appearance of Muslim influence.

30. E. E. Evans-Pritchard, *Witchcraft, Oracles and Magic*, Oxford University Press, 1937, p. 204.

31. Page 690.

32. E. G. Parrinder, *Witchcraft*, London, 1958, p. 128.

33. Dr. L. Swantz writes, "My studies in Dar es Salaam revealed that there are approximately 700 medicine men dealing with 10,000 clients a day." This was written in 1970. He further reports that about one percent of those appearing for mental disorders are considered demented by the medicine men.

34. Parrinder, *op. cit.*, p. 125.

35. Sidney Jourard, *The Transparent Self*, 1964, p. 82.

36. Colossians 2:15.

37. Luke 4:36.

38. Jourard, *op. cit.*, p. 143.

For Further Reading

FROMM, E. *The Art of Loving*, Harper, New York, N.Y., 1956.

JOURARD, SIDNEY. *The Transparent Self*, D. Van Nostrand Co., Inc., Princeton, N.J., 1964.

JUNG, C. G. *Modern Man in Search of a Soul*, Harcourt, Brace, New York, N.Y., 1933.

REIK, T. *Listening with the Third Ear*, Harcourt, Brace, New York, N.Y., 1949.

UNGER, M. F. *Biblical Demonology*, Van Kampen Press, Wheaton, Ill., 1952.

WEATHERHEAD, L. D. *Psychology, Religion, and Healing*, Abingdon, Nashville, Tenn., 1951.

The Author

Donald R. Jacobs was born near Johnstown, Pennsylvania. He received his BA from Franklin and Marshall College, Lancaster, Pennsylvania; MA from the University of Maryland, College Park, Maryland; Diploma of Education from University of London, London, England; and PhD from New York University, New York, New York.

He has taught in the Kentucky public schools (1946-48) and Lancaster Mennonite School, Lancaster, Pennsylvania (1949-52); served as headmaster of the Bumangi Boarding School, Musoma, Tanzania (1954-55); taught at Katoka Teacher Training College, Bukoba, Tanzania (1956-58); and was instructor in Sociology of Religion, New York University (1960-61). He was founder and principal of Mennonite Theological College, Musoma, Tanzania (1961-65). He has also taught at Eastern Mennonite College, Harrisonburg, Virginia, and served as visiting lecturer at

Associated Mennonite Biblical Seminaries, Elkhart, Ind.

He has served as missionary under the Eastern Mennonite Board of Missions and Charities in Tanzania from 1954 to 1966 during which time he was engaged mainly in theological education and church administration. He was ordained to the ministry in 1953 and as bishop for the Tanzanian Mennonite Church in 1964. He was the last American bishop serving in Tanzania from 1964-66.

Since 1966 he has served as Field Secretary for his agency, covering East and Southern Africa. Since 1970 he has been lecturer in African Philosophy and Religion, University of Nairobi, Kenya.

He is author of *History of the Mennonites of Lancaster Conference, 1890-1950* (1953. MA thesis unpublished). *Puberty Ritual and Culture Themes of the Akamba* (1961. Unpublished PhD dissertation); *Christian Theology in Africa, Record of an Experiment* (1966. Nairobi, Kenya); *The Christian Stance in a Revolutionary Age* (1969. Herald Press, Scottdale, Pa. John F. Funk Lecture for 1968).

He has served in various positions of responsibility in connection with the Mennonite mission work in East and Southern Africa. He has been Director of the Summer Institutes on World Mission in the North American Mennonite Church, 1960-70.

Donald R. and Anna Ruth Jacobs are the parents of four children and live in Nairobi, Kenya.